MUSIC AND FASHION

ALISON HAWES

Badger Publishing Limited
Oldmedow Road,
Hardwick Industrial Estate,
King's Lynn PE30 4JJ
Telephone: 01438 791037

www.badgerlearning.co.uk

2 4 6 8 10 9 7 5 3 1

Music and Fashion ISBN 978-1-78147-551-5

Publisher: Susan Ross
Senior Editor: Danny Pearson
Designer: Fiona Grant

Photos: Cover image: REX/Nils Jorgensen
Page 4: Unknown/Daily Mail/REX
Page 6: REX
Page 7: CPL Archv/Everett/REX
Page 8: Everett Collection/REX
Page 9: Lehtikuva OY/REX
Page 11: Courtesy Everett Collection/REX
Page 12: Roger- Viollet/REX
Page 13: DAVID MCENERY/REX & David Graves/REX
Page 14: Richard Posser/REX
Page 15: REX
Page 16: BRIAN ROGERS/REX
Page 17: Courtesy Everett Collection/REX
Page 18: Nils Jorgensen/REX
Page 19: IIpo Musto/REX
Page 20: REX
Page 21: Ken Towner/Associated Newspa/REX
Page 22: Martyn Goddard/REX
Page 23: Sipa Press/REX
Page 24: Sipa Press/REX
Page 25: REX
Page 26: David Swindells/PYMCA/REX
Page 27: Brian Rasic/REX
Page 28: Richard Young/REX
Page 29: Photofusion/REX
Page 30: Beretta/Sims/REX
Page 31: Sipa Press/REX & PictureGroup/REX

Attempts to contact all copyright holders have been made.
If any omitted would care to contact Badger Learning, we will be happy to make appropriate arrangements.

MUSIC AND FASHION

Contents

Badger LEARNING

FORTIES STYLE

Looking like Mum and Dad

In the 1940s, young people, like your great grandparents, would have worn the same sorts of clothes as their mums and dads!

Young women wore fitted dresses or suits, often with a hat and gloves. Their hair would have been long and rolled up or curled.

Young men wore a suit or a shirt and tie. Their hair would have been short at the back and sides and a little longer on top. It was often kept in place with a dab of hair cream.

Making do

For most of the 1940s, the world was at war and clothes were rationed. Everyone had to look after the few clothes they had and make them last. People became good at mending and altering their clothes and making new ones out of recycled fabric.

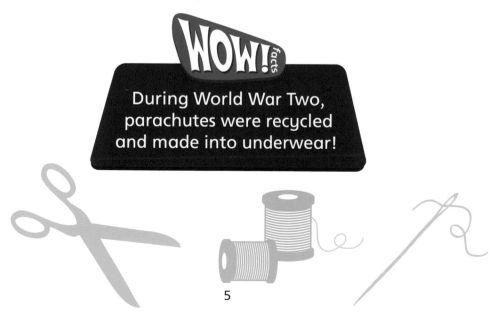

WOW! facts

During World War Two, parachutes were recycled and made into underwear!

FORTIES SOUNDS

Young people in the 1940s listened to music on the radio or played records, called 78s, on a gramophone. They also loved to dance to live music.

The big band sound

The most popular music in the forties was played by bands like the Glenn Miller Orchestra. These 'big bands' had up to 25 members and played a type of jazz music called 'swing'.

The Jitterbug

One of the most popular dances in the 1940s was the Jitterbug. This was a fast partner dance from the USA. It included lifts and acrobatic moves!

The Jitterbug was brought to Europe and Australia by American troops during World War Two.

FIFTIES STYLE

In the 1950s, life began to change. The war was over and rationing came to an end. There was plenty of work and, for the first time, young people had money to spend on themselves.

The first teenagers

The youth of the 1950s were the first real teenagers. They were the first young people to dress in their own style, rather than dressing like their mums and dads.

Fifties teenagers dressed more casually than those in the 1940s. Boys began to wear jeans, T-shirts and leather jackets, like their favourite film stars.

Girls wore tight sweaters or fitted blouses, with cropped trousers or full skirts in bright colours.

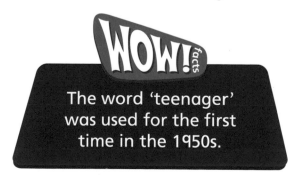

WOW! facts

The word 'teenager' was used for the first time in the 1950s.

FIFTIES SOUNDS

In the 1950s, teenagers crowded around the jukeboxes in coffee bars to hear the latest sounds.

Rock and roll

The most popular music back then was rock and roll. This loud piano or guitar led music began in America. Singers like Elvis Presley and Little Richard made it popular the world over.

The Hand Jive

The Hand Jive was a popular fifties dance that involved lots of different hand moves and claps. You did not need a partner or much room to do it.

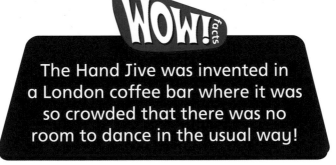

WOW! facts

The Hand Jive was invented in a London coffee bar where it was so crowded that there was no room to dance in the usual way!

ELVIS PRESLEY

MGM's

Jailhouse Rock

CinemaScope

SIXTIES STYLE

The mini

In the 1960s, young people, like your grandparents, had lots of different fashion styles to choose from.

Many of the styles, like the mini skirt, began in the UK and quickly spread across the world.

Mods and Rockers

Two of the most popular sixties styles for young men were very different from each other. Mods wore slim, fitted suits under long green parkas. Their hair was short, neat and layered.

Rockers wore jeans, T-shirts and black leather jackets. Their hair was long on top and kept in place with hair cream.

WOW! facts

In the sixties, fights sometimes broke out between Mods and Rockers!

Hippies

The hippie look became popular in the late sixties. Hippies were anti-fashion. They grew their hair long and wore wide jeans or long skirts, with bright tops and sandals.

SIXTIES SOUNDS

Beatlemania

In the 1960s, The Beatles were the most famous pop group in the world. Along with many other British bands at that time, they became very popular in America and across the world. This became known as the 'British Invasion'.

Wherever The Beatles went they were met by screaming fans.

The Motown Sound

At the same time, American soul and R&B music, sung by groups such as The Four Tops and The Supremes, became very popular in Europe. So much of this music was recorded at Motown Records, in the USA, that it became known as the 'Motown Sound'.

The Twist

The dance craze of the 1960s was the Twist. It all started with a 1960s song, called *The Twist*, by Chubby Checker. Lots of songs with 'twist' in the title followed, including *Twist and Shout* by The Beatles.

WOW! facts

The Beatles have sold over two billion albums and their music still sells today!

SEVENTIES STYLE

Three of the most extreme fashion looks of the 1970s were inspired by the music and bands of that time.

Glam rock

In the early seventies, glam rock bands like T-Rex and Slade were famous for their bright, glittery stage clothes and make-up. Teenagers copied their long hair, wide trousers and platform heels.

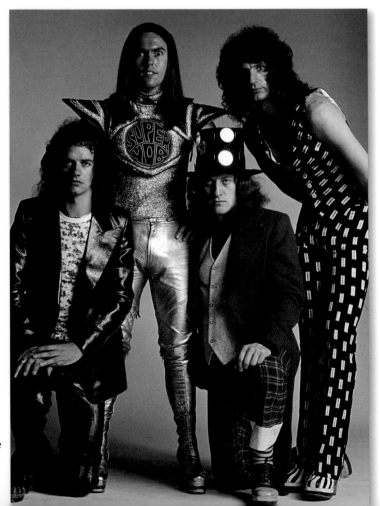

Slade

Disco

A few years later, a craze for disco music swept the world and young people began to dress in style to go disco dancing. Young men wore coloured suits, or shirts with wide lapels and flared trousers. Girls wore frilly dresses, or sparkly tops and jackets.

Punk

In the late seventies, punk music and fashion were popular in Europe, America and Australia. Many punks dressed to shock. They wore dark clothing, decorated with chains, studs and pins. Their hairstyles were extreme, too!

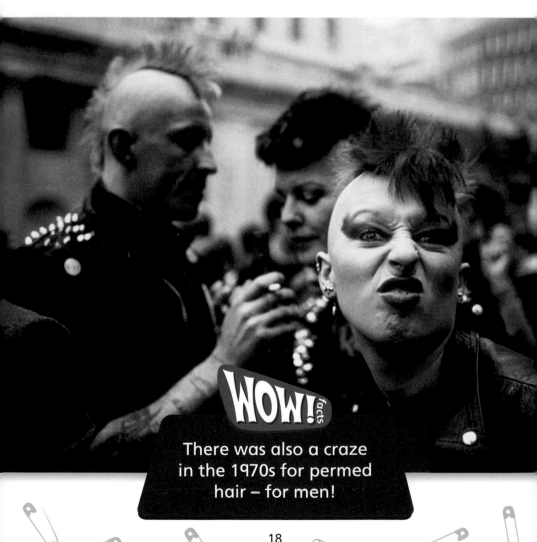

WOW! facts

There was also a craze in the 1970s for permed hair – for men!

SEVENTIES SOUNDS

Glam rock

Glam rock music began in the UK. David Bowie was one of the most well-known musicians of the glam rock era. He was as famous for his music as he was for his make-up and over-the-top clothes.

David Bowie

Disco

The seventies craze for disco music began in the nightclubs of America. It was dominated by black female singers, such as Donna Summer and Gloria Gaynor.

Punk

Punk was a loud and aggressive kind of rock music made famous by bands like The Ramones and The Clash.

The Clash

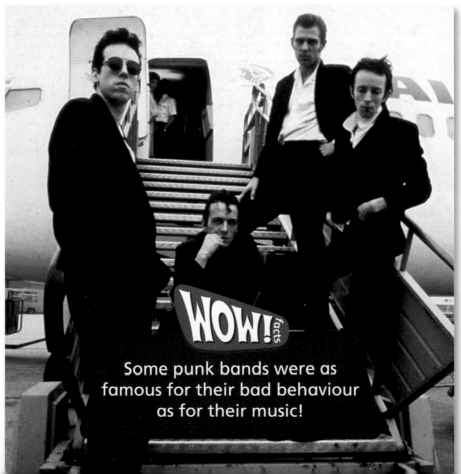

WOW! facts

Some punk bands were as famous for their bad behaviour as for their music!

3. SHOULDER PADS TO SPORTSWEAR

Were your parents teenagers in the 1980s or 1990s?
How cool (or uncool!) did they look then?

EIGHTIES STYLE

The eighties was a time when young men and women
began to dress more like each other.

Girls will be boys

Girls began to wear more masculine
clothes, such as trousers and suits.
Even girls' dresses and jackets were
made to look more masculine with
huge shoulder pads.

Duran Duran were a popular New Romantic band.

Boys will be girls

Young men began to take more interest in how they looked. Many began to wear more feminine colours and patterns. In particular, the New Romantic look of the early eighties had men wearing softer, more feminine clothing and floppy haircuts.

WOW! facts

Skincare products especially for men were first sold in the 1980s.

EIGHTIES SOUNDS

Many of the most successful pop artists of the eighties were solo singers. Two of them, Michael Jackson and Madonna, were known as the King and Queen of Pop.

Madonna

The American singer, Madonna, released her first album in 1983 and is the best-selling female recording artist of all time. She was also known as a fashion icon as well as a pop singer, as many people liked to copy the way she dressed.

Michael Jackson

Michael Jackson began his singing career with his brothers. But he became more famous as a solo artist. His 1982 album, *Thriller*, is the best-selling album of all time.

WOW! facts

Michael Jackson made the moonwalk popular. This was a dance move where he moved backwards while seeming to go forwards!

NINETIES STYLE

Sportswear as streetwear

In the eighties and into the nineties, teenagers began to dress more casually. Teenage boys began wearing sports clothes, such as football shirts and tracksuits, as fashion items.

Hip hop bands, like Run DMC and the Beastie Boys, made wearing sportswear as streetwear cool.

At the same time, sports items, like leggings, leotards and sweatshirts, became popular streetwear for young girls. Just about everyone wore trainers!

Grunge

Grunge also became a popular style in the 1990s.
Ripped or stonewashed jeans and combat trousers were
worn with T-shirts or flannel shirts and work boots. Even
dresses were worn with lace-up boots! Clothes were
loose and comfortable, rather than stylish. The grunge
look was deliberately scruffy and anti-fashion.

WOW! facts

Grunge hair was messy
and untidy, too!

NINETIES SOUNDS

Hip hop and rap

Hip hop music and rap were developed by young black Americans in the 1970s, in New York. But it was in the 1990s that this type of music became popular worldwide.

Artists like Dr Dre and Eminem helped bring rap to a wider audience.

Girl power

During the eighties and nineties, women and girls were becoming more independent. More women than ever were in high-powered jobs and the Spice Girls introduced the world to 'girl power'.

Spice Girls

This British girl band became known all over the world. They sent a message to girls everywhere that they could be strong and loud and have fun!

WOW! facts

The Spice Girls' first album, *Spice*, is the best-selling album by a female group – ever!

4. ONESIES TO ONE DIRECTION

Were you born after 2000? What trends in fashion and music did you notice while growing up in the noughties?

NOUGHTIES STYLE

Young people continued to dress very casually in the noughties. Their look was often based on clothes that were originally worn as work wear or sportswear.

New look jeans

In the mid-2000s, the fashion for wearing skinny jeans began. Coloured jeans were also introduced. Both items were equally popular with girls and boys.

The onesie

A craze for wearing an all-in-one tracksuit, or onesie, began in 2012. These, giant zip-up bodysuits were worn as nightwear or streetwear.

The boys from One Direction wearing onesies.

NOUGHTIES SOUNDS

Few teenagers in the noughties bought music CDs. Instead, they downloaded or streamed the music they liked from the internet.

Megastars

In the early 2000s, the music charts were dominated by megastars, like Kanye West, Jay-Z, Beyoncé and Rihanna.

Boys and girls

Later, many British boy bands, such as One Direction, who were from the reality music show *X Factor*, enjoyed worldwide fame. International female solo singers, from Lady Gaga to Kylie and Adele, also sold millions of records in the noughties.

Adele has won so many awards and broken so many music chart records that she is in the Guinness World Records Book.

WOW! facts

Adele was offered a recording contract when a video of her singing was posted on the internet!

INDEX